ALL I KNOW ABOUT MANAGEMENT I LEARNED FROM MY DOG

ALL I KNOW
ABOUT MANAGEMENT
I LEARNED FROM
MY DOG

MARTIN P. LEVIN

SKYHORSE PUBLISHING

Skyhorse Publishing books may be purchased in bulk at special discounts for sales promotion, corporate gifts, fund-raising, or educational purposes. Special editions can also be created to specifications. For details, contact the Special Sales Department, Skyhorse Publishing, 307 West 36th Street, 11th Floor, New York, NY 10018 or info@skyhorsepublishing.com.

Skyhorse® and Skyhorse Publishing® are registered trademarks of Skyhorse Publishing, Inc.®, a Delaware corporation.

www.skyhorsepublishing.com

10 9 8 7 6 5 4 3 2 1

Library of Congress Cataloging-in-Publication Data is available on file.
ISBN: 978-1-61608-324-3

Printed in China

Cover and page design by Keira McGuinness

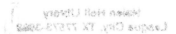

In memory of

Marcia Obrasky Levin

She taught us how to write and what was right.

CONTENTS

CONTENTS

Introduction

When I decided to adopt a dog by the name of Angel, I thought this would be an interesting but not very challenging experience. Bad judgment. I knew almost nothing about her, and it appeared that I was not going to get much help from her. I sought the advice of Paula, my associate and solver of all problems, who had dogs of her own, and she helped - a little. I collected books from every possible source. This also helped - a little.

It soon became clear that my best resource for managing Angel would be, unexpectedly, the six decades of experience I had had in a variety of management positions and the principles I had learned in the process. I began to recall some personal adventures, which added to my insight. And this, in turn, led to recollections about many of the wonderful people who had enriched my professional life, some of whom you already know about, such as the author, Stephen King, and others whom you may be reading about for the first time.

INTRODUCTION

This was supplemented by my previous work assignments among them trips to India in 1956 and 1957 for the Ford Foundation to create a marketing plan for paperback books in the five local languages of South India.

In the case of Angel, it took almost two years of work to achieve the ultimate goal of all management - to help an individual (or dog) achieve her fullest potential. Looking back, it seems that all the complicated advice I was reading was interesting, although much more than I actually needed, as my management style has always been to minimize - that is, to reduce complexity to its basics, to try to put what needs to be done into a single memorable sentence or, better yet, a short and simple phrase.

As it turned out, my journey with Angel led me to four, yes, only four —GOLDEN RULES of management. What had become clear, as the writing of the book progressed, was that many concepts that originally seemed to be distinct were, in fact, interrelated. This resulted in the following:

RULE 1: *Trust & Leadership*

These, it became evident, were really different sides of the same coin. In addition, there was a strong relationship between trust, leadership and excellence.

RULE 2: *Communication*

It became obvious that it was impossible to separate different form of communication - there was a community of spirit: Dog talk led directly to memorable speeches.

RULE 3: *Problem Solving & Decision Making*

These, too, are integrated tasks.

RULE 4: *Perseverance*

This leads inevitably to success.

In the end, the *Four Golden Rules of Management* are so simple that even Angel gets it. If a manager can develop trust, it will lead to corporate excellence, provided he is able to communicate effectively, make the right strategic decisions, and, above all, persevere.

To help you walk the walk that I walked, I have put markers (street signs) in the table of contents so that you can follow the path I traveled.

Welcome to the neighborhood.

PART ONE

Enter Angel

After sixty-eight years of a special marriage, my wife, Marcia, died. I was grieving, and I sought help. As weeks of counseling turned into months, my sage and sympathetic therapist said, "You'll feel better if you get a dog." This mantra was repeated week after week as he would walk me to the door of his office. "You'll feel better if you get a dog," he would say as we parted. I thought to myself disdainfully, I've had a dog; in fact, I've had several dogs. But I've had only one wife, and I'm not convinced that a border collie is going to do the trick, even conceding the devoted loyalty of dogs and the fact they are man's best friend.

Nevertheless, one sunny Sunday I came upon a photograph in the local newspaper that was promoting the "Pet of the Week." I shared the image of the somewhat sad-faced pooch with Paula, who had come into my life as a caregiver for my wife and, despite having a family of her own, signed on as what, in more august circles, would be designated as my "chief of staff." We regarded the photo for some time, until, finally, aware that I was getting a failing grade in grief management, I thought it was at least worth consideration, "Okay," I said, "it won't hurt to take a look."

ALL I KNOW ABOUT MANAGEMENT

Little did I expect, when I was walking down a path of barking dogs crying for attention at the Briarcliff SPCA, that by rescuing Angel, a mature female golden retriever/virgule chow mix, I would be gaining a companion in my eighty-ninth year.

When you adopt a dog from the SPCA, all that you are told is the dog's breed, age (often understated), that it is healthy (often not fully known), and that it has had all its shots. You are not told the name of its previous owner, nor of the circumstances that put it into a holding facility. When you leave with your adopted dog, the SPCA provides you with a leash, a few cans of dog food, and a list of suggestions on how to care for your dog. You are told that the adoption is conditional upon the agency being satisfied that you have adequate facilities and a family setting that will make you a proper owner. On your side, if, after thirty days, you believe that you've made a mistake, you can return the dog.

As I sat in the office, signing the adoption papers, I thought of the major changes that had taken place during my business career. Over a period of six decades, I had changed jobs only four times but the first day on each job was always tense. There was always a worry about whether it would be all I had hoped for. There were new people to meet, concerns about the problems that might arise, and anxiety about whether I was really up to the challenges.

When we left the SPCA with Angel, we felt that, somehow, we had been blessed, even though on that first encounter, Angel did not look what would otherwise be called "her best." Her golden coat was caked with mud, and on the ride back to the house, she sat shivering uncontrollably, crouched on a cover on the backseat of our car. Our repeated cooing of reassurances - "You're a good dog; we love you" - did nothing to stop the tremors. Angel was not a happy dog.

When we arrived at our home, it was like those scenes from *"M*A*S*H"* where the helicopter lands with wounded troops from the front lines and the doctors scramble to save them as best they know how.

I dashed out to Petco to get the essentials: a cage in which Angel would sleep, cans of proper dog food, and a few toys. Until then, I had not felt as if I was involved in a flurry of activities akin to preparing immediately after taking one's firstborn home from the hospital. Now I did.

Paula remained behind at the house, dragging a reluctant Angel down the hall for a bath. She wrestled Angel into my late wife's bathtub (I hope my wife was not watching from above, as I can assure the reader that she would not have liked this one bit). Paula needed all the strength she could muster to engineer the bath, because Angel was a big, strong dog, weighing then over fifty-seven pounds, a weight that seemed at the time the upper limit a dog should reach and now, after the years of nourishment and outright indulgence that have followed, puts Angel, in comparison, into the lapdog category (her current weight remains a state secret).

As she lathered Angel with soap, Paula soon discovered that, while bred as a water dog, Angel absolutely despised being bathed. Angel tried repeatedly to climb out of the tub and, when she could not get any traction, sent up plumes of water, drenching Paula. Finally, when Angel was lifted out of the tub, she followed the protocol of all dogs when wet and shook herself off with a mighty series of shakes, covering Paula with soapy water from head to toe.

Still, in spite of it all, when I came home from my shopping, I saw, instead of the scruffy, shaking animal I had left behind with Paula, a beautiful dog with a silky golden coat. Angel looked up at me, her big brown eyes framed by blond circles of hair, standing elegantly, proudly, alongside a smiling (and drenched) Paula.

I unpacked Angel's new twin dishes and filled one with water and the other with Petco's best cuisine. However, instead of rushing to the food dishes as I had expected, Angel stood frozen, watching us intently. She moved slowly to her dishes, smelled around the edges of the food dish, turned to see where we were, moved toward the food, ran her nose around the rim of the dish, and then ate ravenously, looking up intermittently to see where we were. After eating, she moved over to the corner of the kitchen, never taking her eyes off us, and rested. It had been, one could easily surmise, in spite of our extraordinary caregiving, a traumatic day for Angel. A nap was in order.

When it was time for bed, we opened the door to the sleeping crate I had purchased, an obvious indication (at least to us) that Angel was to go inside. There was absolutely no movement on Angel's part. We attempted sweet talk: "You are a good girl, lovely angel, sweet Angel." This also produced no movement. Angel's immobility made it clear that she had no interest whatsoever in sleeping in a crate. It sent a clear message to us that she needed (and would insist upon) freedom, but, even more, it seemed that closed areas frightened her. Whether this was on account of her confinement at the shelter - the duration of which unknown to us - or the result of some earlier trauma, or merely a personality trait, we were never to know, although in the days to come, we did learn enough about her earlier history to lead us to a good guess.

Finally, Paula found a mat and put it alongside her bed. Angel approached the mat slowly, cautiously settled down on that mat, rested her nose across her left paw, and went to sleep. I have no idea where that crate is now (another of Paula's magic maneuvers, I suspect), but I know for certain the it is no longer in my house. Currently, Angel, who enjoys naps during the day, sleeps at my feet when I am working at home, and at night, she sleeps in Paula's room on a large comfortable mattress sufficient for her now well-fed bulk.

Our challenge was that, without any knowledge of Angel's previous life, we had to establish a role in Angel's life, to be her leader, gain her respect and love, and bring out Angel's stored potential in order to help her solve problems, make decisions, and acquire attributes that would make ours a productive relationship. Not having knowledge of what had gone on in her life before we arrived on the scene meant that we had to probe (gently but persistently) to discover what she already knew and then build on this base.

It was only after we pressed the SPCA that we learned Angel had a history that explained our difficult early adventures. Angel had spent her early years with a family, had run away, roamed in a wooded area, lived outdoors for many months, had been given occasional asylum by home owners in the area, had taken shelter in storms, had found food wherever she could, and had fought off other animals who threatened her. Eventually, she was found by the dog rescuers. The SPCA located her owners and offered to return her to the family, but the wife refused to take Angel back because her husband had abused the dog. This history was enough to know that we had our work cut out for us. It would be a slow and delicate process.

And, as the process continued with Angel, step by step, I found that what I was doing was startlingly similar to what had occurred in my management career, which spanned over six decades. Working with Angel, day by day, brought it all back: the ten years in public service, the seventeen years in trade-book publishing, and the seventeen years as CEO, rebuilding a major diversified publishing company - all this to be followed, at the age of sixty-one, by obtaining a law school degree (while continuing to manage a publishing company) in order, finally, to achieve my childhood dream of one day becoming an attorney. This second (or, perhaps, third or fourth) career as a publishing attorney, buying and selling publishing companies for clients, teaching publishing and intellectual-property law at a New York City law school, is now in its twenty-fifth year and every day brings a reassurance that, with persistence, I can accomplish what I set out to do - no matter how difficult the circumstances.

Unexpectedly, I have found that my daily interactions with Angel, the frightened, unknown, and once-abandoned dog, have given me both the inspiration and the challenge to reacquaint myself with those essential management principles that have guided my professional and now my private life (both canonical and canine-ical), and have led to the decision to share these with you, the reader.

I find that in facing a new problem, my brain scrambles to find bits of knowledge that have been stored away. It is only after the fact that I realize what old information I have used to solve the new problem. When I needed Angel to trust me,

I unconsciously reached back, recalling the first meeting with the staff in a failing company. They were looking at me to save their jobs. I knew then, as I would learn anew with Angel, that first I had to gain their trust. The techniques I used then to accomplish a feeling of trust came off the shelf of my memory. If this is not convincing, let me refer you to Yogi Berra, the former all-star baseball catcher and sage, who would describe this process as *déjà vu* all over again."

It is my hope that the reader will find some wisdom, some humor, and perhaps even a great story here and there - some mine and some borrowed and tucked away for this special occasion. I have taken the liberty of providing some photographs of Angel along with the text, not only to offer the opportunity to look inspiration squarely in the muzzle but to establish, undisputedly, what a very pretty dog she is.

Say No to Drugs

I am not sure who created the management doctrine, but it contains the principle of "unintended consequences," which holds that in trying to do good things, bad things may happen. The event described below falls squarely within the ambit of this doctrine.

Very early in our relationship, I needed to take Angel with me on her first airplane ride. Angel was certified as a service dog, and this permitted her to fly in the main cabin of the aircraft and occupy a seat beside me, or, as she preferred, to stretch out on the floor in front of her assigned (and purchased) seat.

Prior to this airborne excursion, Angel had to be examined by a veterinarian and certified as "fit to fly." I thought that given the trust we had been developing between us, she would feel comfortable with me and Paula, who by now had become Angel's best friend. However, the vet, to be safe, gave us some Xanax. Yes, this is the same drug used by humans for anxiety, suggesting still another bond between man and dog. The medication could be given, I was informed by the vet, should Angel become anxious in flight (something I should have known by now would be a given). The recommended dosage was up to two pills for a three-hour trip.

Angel was fine for the first half hour, but, as the airplane gained altitude, she began to shake. We gave her one half of a pill. No visible change. We waited about a half hour; the shaking got worse. We gave her the other half of the pill. And, after another half hour, with no abatement of the shaking, we gave her the second pill.

The shaking stopped and Angel, on the floor near the seat, slept peacefully - one might say like an angel, although, on reflection, I can't say I've ever actually seen a sleeping angel, even in the abundant depictions of them in Renaissance art. And there on the floor, throughout the remainder of flight, Angel stayed, all seventy-one pounds of her (I guess I've let the "dog out of the bag," so to speak, but we accepted a twenty-five percent weight gain as a measure of our success and her happiness, in spite of

Angel's becoming ever closer to resembling a small keg rather than a large canine).

As we neared the end of the flight, we decided the time had arrived to awaken Angel so that we might leave the aircraft. No movement. No response to her name. Nothing. The airplane began its descent. We got a bottle of water and dampened her face with a cloth. Nothing. Angel was dreaming the kind of dreams only dogs can love, and from which no dog wishes to be interrupted.

The airplane landed. No movement from Angel, who gave all the indications of having become embedded in the aircraft. The plane emptied. We were the only passengers on board. The captain of the airplane came back to evaluate the situation. Seeing the snoozing Angel, and being trained in enterprising maneuvers, he sent for a wheelchair. The chair rolled down the aisle and came to a stop at Angel, who had become a testimonial to the marvels of modern pharmacology, undeniably anxiety-free - but also still unconscious.. With not a small amount of effort, the three of us managed to pick up this huge snoring animal. (Her owners had allowed her to balloon to seventy-one pounds!) We carried her to the exit door and loaded her on to the wheelchair. Angel, still sleeping, slipped about in the wheelchair as an airline employee pushed it along. Her front paws hung off one side, her hind legs off the other side, and her head drooped off the seat Paula stood by to make certain Angel did not totally dislodge from the rolling handicap apparatus.

Did I mention that Angel was in her full service-dog regalia wearing a large white bib with a giant red cross on it so there would be no doubt that she was fully certified to provide a full range of assistance to her disabled owner? Probably not.

However, as we walked through the airport, people did stop now and then to take in the sight of a giant golden retriever, a well-decorated service dog, being rolled through the airport on a wheelchair, accompanied by a lady dashing from side to side to avoid "slippage," keeping the dog from tumbling to the ground and being, in essence, run over by her own nonambulatory device, behind which trudged an old guy, who might very well have been the owner of the dog, laden with several heavy bags and attempting to keep up with his dormant aide.

We finally loaded Angel, still sleeping, into our car for the ride to our home in Sarasota, stopping en route at a

PetSmart to have the vet on duty exam her. He pronounced her fit (I believe the word he used was "alive") and said Angel would, "in due time," though he was no more specific than this, sleep it off.

However, our excursion was not yet finished. We still needed to get Angel, who was laid out on the backseat of our car like one of those bear rugs one finds in hunting lodges, out of the vehicle and up and into my sixth-floor apartment.

Fortunately, there was a luggage cart available on the first floor. Angel, still out cold in a way known, I suspect, only to those who have had the misfortune of getting into the ring with Muhammad Ali, was finally rolled onto the luggage cart as the heads of residents poked from balconies above and looked down at this animal with a giant red-cross bib sprawled on the luggage cart, we wheeled Angel into the building, rode up the elevator, finally entered my apartment, and, by tilting the baggage cart, deposited Angel on the floor next to my bed.

About four hours after we landed, Angel awoke, still groggy, and made it known that she had the need to go outside and relieve herself. Heads reappeared on the balconies (word spreads fast in my condo complex when something as worthy of attention as this occurs) to watch and speculate about an old guy accompanying a "service" dog who looked staggeringly drunk, and who alternately peed and collapsed, was pulled to an upright position, peed some more, collapsed some more, was uprighted again, and so on, until her business was at last accomplished.

The next morning, as though the events of the previous day had never occurred, Angel was herself, ready with her usual "O What a Wonderful Morning" energy, perhaps even more than usual, as she seemed extraordinarily well rested for an animal of her age and girth.

Angel has been on an airplane many times since. According to expert opinion, she probably does not remember that first episode. The same can, obviously, not be said about her owner, his chief of staff, and, perhaps, a significant number of others who witnessed various portions of this event. However, we no longer medicate. We count on the respect and trust she has for us. Sometimes she shakes, but she knows that all will be well. This is a lesson both of us have learned.

In a management context, getting good advice from an expert when facing a new experience is very sound.

However, in dealing with unknowns such as tolerance levels, the manager uses his best judgment, and should be ready to accept the unpredictable consequences. The resourceful manager should be able to deal with an uncomfortable result and place the event in the "do not repeat" file. The expert should not be faulted because this event was out of his control. He should, however, limit the medication to a dose that in the end will not cause any serious harm. There is a message here for both the consultant and the actor.

Hitting the Books

After the airplane adventure with Angel, I decided to hit the books to learn more about her and her ancestors. My early experiences with dogs were obviously well out-of-date. After reading a number of books and researching on the Web, I put together a short summary, updating the modest amount I knew, which gave credence to the extraordinary contributions that dogs make to humans.

According to the experts, dogs are descended from wolves and may have been domesticated for 135,000 years. While this time line may be a stretch, there are clear references to dogs in ancient Greek writings. Homer, composing the *Odyssey*, it is surmised, in the eight or ninth century B.C., says, "As they were talking, a dog that had been lying asleep raised his head and pricked up his ears." This image of a sleeping dog who rises up and pricks his ears is pure Angel, spanning the time divide, and is as relevant today as it was in the time of the ancient Greeks.

Having established the long relationship (and companionship?) to man, I sought to find out how a dog's brain works. Researchers report that although the brain of the average dog accounts for only .5 percent of its body weight (as compared to 2 percent in the average human and .07 percent in most other mammals), a dog's brain is able to synthesize, interpret, and act upon an extraordinary amount of information it receives from its senses. Since the brain needs a great deal of nourishment to function properly (it gets 20 percent of the blood pumped from the heart), Angel, who, as has been established by now, has a passion for food, especially table food, must have a well-nourished and healthy heart.

Brain activity is, in part, predetermined by "fixed wiring" provided by the genes. As human brains are prewired for language, so is a dog's brain prewired to interpret scents, a large part of the brain being devoted to this process. Of course, the brain also processes information from all the other senses - touch, taste, hearing, and sight. However, what dogs lack that humans have is an abundant capacity for association, so a dog often looks to humans for guidance in decision making and how to avoid danger.

A dog's brain can, as determined by genetics, store conditioned or learned information. Composed of billions of cells (neurons), each of which may have ten thousand connectors through various neurotransmitters and receptor sites, a dog's brain is quite similar anatomically to the brains of other mammals. As in humans and other mammals, the cerebrum controls emotions and behavior, while the cerebellum controls muscle activity. Even though emotions in a dog may be limited, experts generally agree that dogs can express these feelings in a manner that has allowed them to communicate successfully with humans for millennia. As only one of many examples, when Paula is away for an extended period and returns, Angel greets her with delight, running around, going for her toys and bringing them to Paula. Under the same circumstance, I get a much more restrained greeting - it's not exactly clear why. One can hypothesize that for Angel this may be the result of her having been abused by a male owner, or it could simply be that Angel likes Paula better. I attribute this entirely to the manner in which Paula prepares Angel's lamb chops.

The brain stem connects to the peripheral nervous system, each sense feeding into the brain through its own unique dedicated network of nerves. A specific region of the brain (the limbic system) integrates instinct and learning, giving emotional value to what we sense and what we learn. Lamb chops are a good thing; baths are not for Angel.

But what about those things that require "empathic" connections? Lamb chops taste good immediately. Baths feel bad immediately. What about lying quietly while your owner is in the midst of an important business call? This is, as every dog owner quickly learns, where dog biscuits enter the picture. Modifying certain aspects of Angel's behavior solely because of her associational limitations requires patient teaching (and dog biscuits). The good news is that most dogs are quick studies, and they learn quickly what must be done to earn a treat. At times, it seems as though Angel has trained me to give treats more than I have trained her to do the act necessary to earn them. Nevertheless, I am never without a supply of treats.

As is true of many other mammals, dogs have their unique characteristics, as well. They have a strong sense of homing, often traveling long distances on land and water to return to their home. Since their eyes are flatter than humans', they can change the shape of the lenses, allowing them to be more sensitive to light and movement than a human, although their resolving power is less efficient.

The mobility of a dog's ears allows it to scan the environment for sound. A dog can hear sounds four times farther away than a human and can locate the sources of the sound in six-hundredths of a second. It appears that Angel, a quiet, loving dog, barks well before we hear that a stranger is at our front door or we hear the first sound of thunder.

Touching is very important in to dogs and humans alike. It is the first sense a dog develops, and it remains powerfully important. There are touch-sensitive hairs, called vibrissae, especially above the eyes, on the muzzle, and below the jaws. A dog's entire body, including its paws, is covered with touch-sensitive nerve endings. Angel's heaven, as is true with most family dogs, is a belly rub. I am a strong believer that, from an emotional standpoint, the human gets as much pleasure from petting a dog as the dog gets in being petted and I suspect that the dog figures that out very quickly.

While dogs have fewer taste buds than humans, approximately one for every six of ours, they still have an ample supply to register sweet, sour, bitter, and salty tastes. With yards of shelves of different dog foods being offered in the supermarkets, the manufacturers have certainly figured this out and have become extraordinarily adept at exploiting (and profiting from) this. Unfortunately, they have not yet developed a food that caters to Angel's highly specialized taste buds, her favorite food being rotisserie chicken (white meat only).

The dog's sense of smell is legendary. Within their two nostrils, there are about two hundred million receptor cells, depending upon the breeds as compared with five million for humans. In sniffing, a task at which Angel excels, she is able to bring molecules into contact with a superior olfactory epithelium, in which the receptor cells are found. Not only do dogs have a strong selectivity and specificity of smells but they can store and recall an extraordinary number of them, as well.

ALL I KNOW ABOUT MANAGEMENT

As previously noted, dogs make relatively few decisions alone; they look to humans to sort it all out for them. Yet they make the most of what they have. *Animals in Translation,* by Temple Grandin, has an elegant explanation of the three-brain theory and how the larger neocortex in humans enables us to process information that a dog cannot. On the other hand, as sophisticated as the human brain is (and brain researchers believe it is becoming even more so), they are often weak where dogs are strong. Military dogs have been very important in protecting our soldiers in Iraq. Welsh Springer spaniels are trained to sniff out incendiary bombs in Iraq. Beagles at airports are able to detect drugs brought into the country illegally. Seeing Eye dogs escort their charges through crowded Manhattan streets and through traffic. Hospice dogs give comfort to the terminally ill. Dogs protect local police. Dogs have been known to rescue the drowning and to find the lost. And there are dogs who are now able to detect the imminent onset of hypoglycemia in diabetics. Of course, their survival skills are also exceptionally strong. Angel, who is now my service dog, had enough decision-making capacity to escape from an abuser, stay on her own for four months, find food, protect herself, and locate shelter in inclement weather. The decision-making capacity for survival had been hardwired into her brain and is part of her heritage.

Armed with this very modest understanding of the history and physiology of dogs, I set about reaching out to Angel to see how far I could get with what originally was this unknown quantity that appeared in my life, much as a manager might find himself encountering a new, largely unknown organization to manage. The management approach that I had been utilizing for over half a century was to learn as much as I could and then use what I had learned to achieve the goals of a successful business - one that would help those involved to achieve their full potential. Given Angel's limitation and advantages, I settled on a select number of issues that were important. The road we traveled took two years, and we're still counting, but I realized that I had traveled this road before, both as follower and leader. How hard could it be?

While there are many permutations, in the end it became apparent that there were only four basic rules that would work for Angel, the same rules that were extracted from six decades of successful management.

PART TWO

The Four Golden Rules of Management

RULE 1

Trust & Leadership

Trust

I t immediately became clear that I had to earn Angel's trust and respect, and build on this, in order for her to achieve her full potential. The dog who shook convulsively in the back of the car en route to our house from the shelter needed the basics: good food, a comfortable bed, lots of walking, and protection from the elements. Bonding would come later.

While Angel and Paula were girlfriends, I never quite made the cut. To do so required an extraordinary gesture. When a burr lodged in her paw on a walk down our sandy road, and I saw she was limping, I stopped and had her turn on her side while I took out the burr. Instinctively, she said "thank you" with a sloppy kiss - a rare sign of affection. She is, after all, a female dog and, it has become apparent, not entirely happy with men. I am not saying that this was a begrudging expression of appreciation, only that it seemed that there was an understanding that this kind of

41

response was reserved only for extraordinary acts of kind-ness on my part.

In the world of humans and the workplace, trust is achieved in part by providing for basic needs, security, and the opportunity for an employee to achieve his or her full potential. Some stroking helps, as well. Unfortunately, with the worst economic depression in the country's history, with high unemployment, reckless investing, and the bank-ruptcy of many major corporations, some measure of trust has understandably eroded. It's become a lot less clear who is looking out for whose interests. The new challenge for managers now is to redouble efforts to restore this trust.

Angel believes there is hope. She points to her own story, which has been described previously. Then Paula and I came along. She is now the prettiest, healthiest, although margin-ally obese, fourteen year-old in the neighborhood. No longer shaking as she approaches the backseat of a car, she jumps in eagerly, landing neatly on the seat, and pokes her nose out of the back window, looking at dogs we pass, dogs walking as she rides by them, her tongue hanging out, her eyes bright. One can imagine her thinking, Look at me. Could any mixed-breed mutt be happier? I seriously doubt it. I don't suppose she attributes this better life to our mutual trust, but I know it's there, and I know that it has provided the deepest foundation, one that has made all other things possible.

Leadership

LEADERS COME IN ALL SIZES AND SHAPES. IN THE EARLY DAYS of working with Angel, I found Cesar Millan through his books and television shows. He is a saint for those owners with problem dogs. Cesar runs the Dog Psychology Center in South Central Los Angeles. His theory is that dogs are pack animals and that they need an alpha person to integrate them into the pack. Each morning, he collects as many as forty dogs behind him and leads the pack on a four-hour walk. If the little dogs get tired, Cesar loads them on the backs of the big dogs. His theory is "Exercise and food . . . work and treats."

There are management counterparts to Cesar's approach. The tough-love component is advocated by many managers, perhaps the most notable proponent being Jack Welch, who claims on the jacket of his best-selling book that he is the "the World's Greatest Business Leader." To be sure, Welch is credited with transforming the General Electric

Company, an aging electronics manufacturer beset by foreign competition, to a world-class company. Welch is known for the dissemination of challenging quotes, a kind of Poor Richard's Almanac for discouraged businessmen. One of his most intriguing aphorisms is his definition of his job as the top boss of General Electric: "I firmly believe my job is to walk around with a can of water in one hand and a can of fertilizer in the other and make things flourish."

In fairness to Welch, putting aside his delight in uttering an almost endless number of pithy antiestablishment quotes, to my mind he certainly got it right where values, transparency, and setting high standards are concerned. At the end of his career at GE, his only job from the time he finished college until he retired, he was named by *Fortune* magazine the CEO of the century. Welch, in Cesar Millan terms, is the alpha male of big business.

One of my mentors, the late Albert V. Casey, was the president of the Times Mirror Company. In 1966, he hired me to be the CEO of a struggling group of publishing companies owned by Times Mirror. (With Al's guidance and some very talented associates, we made this struggling entity the fifth-largest publisher in the United Staes and very profitable.) Al and I worked together for eight years, until American Airlines reached out to make him its CEO in 1974. He replaced the legendary C. R. Smith, the founder of American Airlines.

Al Casey was a graduate of the Harvard Business School, the holy grail of all business schools. In the face of the classic Harvard curriculum, Casey reduced management to its essentials. For example, to have a successful company, Casey believed that you need only four individuals: "a person making the stuff, a person to sell the stuff, a bean counter to keep score, and a boss." In addition to reducing complex matters to the essentials, he did it with a sly Irish wit (the result of kissing the Blarney Stone every now and again, he might say).

Al accepted monumental challenges when he became CEO at American Airlines, and he cautioned his wife, Ellie, not to expect him home for a while. He then proceeded to fly every route that American flew, talked to the crews on board and in the ready rooms. This was Casey's style - managing was about "walking around." People were never sure when Al would appear, but they knew that he would be around in person, even if it was for just a short visit, to see for himself how they were doing. By walking around, he always obtained valuable unfiltered information directly from employees and customers. His presence in the field also demonstrated that he really cared. He was able to discuss and arrive at shared goals by sitting in ready rooms with pilots, crew, and ground staff, as well as his executives, in the boardroom. By talking bluntly about financial performance, and the problems they all faced, he developed trust and demonstrated transparency. Al warned that there would be mistakes before they got it right and that this, too, was part of the process. No matter the difficulty of the problem, all he asked was the sharing of information with no surprises. It was typical of Al to create a new "Casey's Law" in his autobiography: "If something can go right, it should."

Murphy's Law tells us that if something can go wrong, it will. "Nonsense!" said Al Casey. But for those things that can go right to do so, Casey maintained that you've got to make them go right, with hard work, by focusing on key problems, and, perhaps most of all, by believing in the people around you. One of the most successful and original American businessmen of our time, Al Casey was a no-nonsense turnaround specialist who loved nothing more than the big challenges, whether in the private or the public sector. As president of Times Mirror Corporation, he was instrumental in taking an historic West Coast company, whose main product was the *Los Angeles Times*, and turning it into a multifaceted media giant, with interests in magazines, newspapers, book publishing, forest products, radio, and television. He presided over Times Mirror's move from a private to a public company, listed first on the NASDAQ and then on the New York Stock Exchange, during his tenure.

As chairman of American Airlines for eleven years, he took that ailing giant heavily in debt and losing money when he became CEO early in 1974 and made it into the highly profitable, preeminent company it still is today. As postmaster general of the United States, he attacked the problems of the country's largest government agency with almost a million employees and left it leaner, more motivated, for the first time truly competitive, and to the great surprise of Washington insiders both efficient and profitable.

Casey's style of management contrasts with Jack Welch in that Casey was a collaborative and decisive manager, while Welch was "top down." Both were effective. It is true that management comes in all sizes and shapes, and new styles are being introduced regularly. The latest contribution to the art of management one with a softer style appears in a new book, *Leading with Kindness*, written by William Baker and Michael O'Malley. The best way to describe this is to share, with the permission of the authors, a fable that describes their management approach.

> A child and his father are hiking. They come upon a long suspension bridge that traverses a deep canyon. It gently swings in the wind that traverses the canyon. The father looks at the boy and says, "We need to get to the other side." The father steps out first and walks a few paces before turning. "Come on walk close to me." The child pauses. "Come on. We have to get to the other side, and I am not going on without you." The boy steps on the bridge and freezes as he feels it shake. The father explains the bridge will shake a little, but their bodies will move quite naturally with it. They start up again. As they near the half way point, the bridge's movements seem soothingly rhythmic and the wind warmly refreshing against their faces. The father stops at the midpoint: "Do you want to lead?" The boy beams with pleasure. "Sure," the boy responds. And they proceed to the other side.

The authors point out that good leadership is like leading people across a suspension bridge. First, the person has to feel secure enough to step on the bridge and start out, to trust that the leader would be there for him and not let him down. They point to development theorists who define this as providing a "secure base" the "safe haven" concept. Second, the endeavor has to be valuable enough to be worth the risk. Third, despite the danger, the leader must convey confidence that, even with fears and unknown consequences, they will press on. Fourth, the leader must ensure that ultimately the experience will be an enjoyable one, so that followers will cross the bridge again, and again bringing their followers back.

Trust, Respect, Leadership

Trust, respect, and leadership (along with a little love) are the bedrock of excellent companies. In Search of Excellence, by Thomas Peters and Robert H. Waterman, Jr., is the seminal book on corporate excellence. Their book expands on the study of seventy-five companies. Their findings are sound. They list eight characteristics that make for excellence in companies:

ALL I KNOW ABOUT MANAGEMENT

1. **Bias for action, for getting on with it.**
   Do it, fix it, and get on with it.

2. **Stay close by your customer.**
   Learn from them. Provide unparalleled quality, service, and reliability.

3. **Autonomy and entrepreneurship.**
   Encourage practical risk taking and support good ideas.

4. **Productivity through People.**
   People are our best investment;
   help them to be more productive.

5. **Hands-on; value driven.**
   This is the Casey mantra: management by walking around.

6. **Stick to the knitting.**
   Stay close to the business you know.

7. **Simple form; lean staff.**
   Keep top level staff small; push authority down to the operating level.

8. **Simultaneous "loose- tight" properties.**
   Centralize only what works.

The findings for the study were based on investigations done in the winter of 1979 and 1980. The contemporary model meeting Peters and Waterman eight points today is Google, founded by Larry Page and Sergey Brin while they were students at Stanford University in Palo Alto,

California. Google was founded as a privately held company in September 1998 and completed its first public offering in August 2004, raising $1.6 billion. *Fortune* magazine lists Google each year at the top or close to the top in its study of the best companies for which to work in the United States, and it is recognized as one of the most powerful brands in the world.

Google's Web-search engine is the most widely used browser on the internet, with well over 50 percent of the market share, with its nearest competitor, Yahoo, slightly under 20 percent. Checking Google's performance against the eight points of excellence, it is clear they get a high grade in every area.

Google, by internal growth, acquisitions, and partnerships, has used its staff and resources to discover areas of growth. It is a restless company, reaching out to make the impossible possible. Google has spent years and appears close to realizing its goal of putting all books previously and currently published online and accessible throughout the world.

The company has stayed close to its customers by meeting needs outside its original product, a search engine, by providing e-mail that has 146 million customers monthly, Web pages, global tracking, and storage for text and for video, and it is now looking seriously at entering the field of mobile technology. Google's headquarters are in Mountain View, California; the company calls the site the Googleplex. In sharp contrast to traditional offices, the Googleplex is a campus. It is a delight to visit. The lobby is decorated with a piano, lava lamps, old server clusters, and a projection of search queries on the wall. The hallways are filled with exercise balls and bicycles.

There are recreational activities scattered throughout the campus amenities include video games, pool tables, weight and rowing machines, and a wide variety of diversions to encourage employees to take a break. As a motivation technique, all Google engineers are encouraged to spend 20 percent of their time (one day a week) on projects of their own. An analysis by Google showed that about half of the new product launches came out of this time-off program.

In addition to Google's substantial Mountain View premises, there is a Google engineering and advertising office in midtown Manhattan. This office has been responsible for over one hundred engineering projects, including Google spreadsheets. In late 2006, Google also opened offices in Pittsburgh and Ann Arbor to make local university resources and talent pools available. This is an excellent example of not being held hostage to one area and its resources, of spreading out and locating advantageously.

In true Google style, the company engineered a novel and primitive approach to a contemporary problem - the environment. Google was challenged about the massive use of energy required to fuel its servers, which are located throughout the world. As part of its response in 2009, Google deployed herds of goats at Googleplex, helping to forestall the threat from seasonal bush fires while also reducing the carbon footprint in mowing the extensive grounds. There is much more to the Google story, and it is told in depth by Ken Auletta in his worthwhile book *Googled: The End of the World as We Know It.*

In Florida, I was reminded that there are millions of small businesses - not just the General Electrics, American Airlines, or Googles of the world - that have established trust and respect and have achieved excellence through strong leadership.

ALL I KNOW ABOUT MANAGEMENT

Every winter, I relocate my office to Sarasota, Florida, where I shop at a fishing and boating supply store named C.B.'s (initials of the founder). The store is about fifteen hundred square feet. It fronts on a major highway and has a rear access from a well-paved two-lane road. There is direct access on one side of the store to the Intercoastal Waterway. C.B. believed in keeping it simple with several huge tanks with shrimp and other live bait. When C.B. sold out, the new owner made improvements over the years. Since there was direct access to the waterway, she built docks so the store could be accessed by boaters. She redesigned the store and moved the bait and lure area into a quarter of the space. In the other space, she created an upscale clothing area for men and women, along with offering small boating equipment, such as life preservers, oars, anchors, fish finders, and so on. And she did all this without renting new space.

Over the years, she built a team of dedicated, knowledgeable employees who had the ability to serve customers, whether they were there to buy bait or the most fashionable boating jacket. Her employees were trained to offer, without charge, the store's most indispensable product: information. Providing advice on where and when to fish, the best gear, the best suntan lotion, the best restaurant along the waterway to stop for lunch, this service represents a virtual Google. Small businesses following the same rules that the giant conglomerates use are successful and are regarded as the "backbone of the U.S. economy."

RULE 2

Communication

DOG TALK

Take My Mule, Please

This is a true story. In late 1955, I was the vice president of Sales for a venerable trade publisher, Grosset & Dunlap. I was invited to lunch by James ("Jay") Laughlin, the owner and publisher of New Directions, a small but prestigious publisher. As a young publisher, I was flattered to have lunch with one of the most interesting publishers in New York, someone who had published the works of Ezra Pound, Dylan Thomas, and Wallace Stevens. Jay said that he had been retained by the Ford Foundation to head up a project in India to assist the Southern Languages Book Trust in creating a mass-market distribution system for books written in the five major languages of South India. This was intended to be a demonstration project and chart a path for the National Book Trust, sponsored by the Indian government. Jay said I had been recommended as an expert and problem solver. The Ford Foundation had allocated $500,000 for this project. In 1955, this was a substantial sum. When I asked why such a major amount had been allocated to translating and distributing books in a country with major food delivery, population control, and health problems, Jay said that the Russian propagandists had made strong inroads in the South of India by printing a variety of books in the local languages and sending them to their Communist cells in South India at no cost, allowing the members of each Communist cell to sell them to the public to raise funds for political action.

I was flattered by the opportunity to serve, but when I heard that if I accepted the assignment, I would be going in April 1956 for six weeks and then back again for a period of evaluation in 1957, I said this would be impossible.

I was on a fast track at Grosset, hoping for promotion. I had two small children and a wife.

Before he left, Jay, making one last try, offered to send my wife with me. I still said no. At dinner that night, I casually mentioned this lunch to my wife, Marcia, whose reaction startled me. She said, "You call him back and tell him we are going. I have always dreamed of going to India. I will call my mother and she will be delighted to stay with the children."

In the end, after some serious reluctance on the part of the chairman of the board of Grosset, who felt that the distribution of books was not a priority for India, and the kindness of Marcia's mother and the support from departmental heads, we left for India in March 1957. To put this date in some perspective, this was less than ten years after India gained its independence from Britain, following over three hundred years of British rule. It would still be four more years before Portugal would give up its colonization in other parts of India.

City names have changed since I was there, but I will be using the names used in 1957 and 1958. We arrived in Delhi after a long flight, with intermediate stops in Shannon, Ireland, and Rome. After a briefing from the Ford Foundation director in Delhi, we flew to Madras in a

DC-3 prop plane. The distance between the two cities is comparable to the distance between New York City and Denver, Colorado. While Delhi was a major center, Madras, the gateway to the south, was a modest-size verdant community with the omnipresent sacred cows parading in the streets. There was one hotel for tourists, the Oceanic, and we occupied the only air-conditioned room. Tamil was the language of the people. The British had left a legacy of English as the language of commerce. Hindi, the national language, was not in common use.

My task was to learn as much as I could about the Indian publishers. I sought the assistance of the chairman of the Southern Language Trust to organize meetings with publishers throughout the south, and so, in the first ten days, I met with large and small publishers throughout South India. There was a unanimity of advice from the publishers. They had their own ideas of how this stimulus package should be used. "Give us the money to print books, because the banks will not lend to us," they said. They reported that the banks' position was that once ink was placed on blank paper (something they felt was a good asset that could be sold in case of a default), the blank paper would be worthless and they would have no collateral. The publisher's proposal was that they be given the Ford Foundation's money to use wisely in order to create sales staffs, buy equipment, and print paperbacks. They promised to meet and defeat the Russian competition.

Giving the money to the Indian publishers had many disadvantages. How much to give to each publisher? What control would we have as to the use of the funds? How would we check to see if Ford was getting the benefit of creating an indigenous ongoing enterprise? I decided to try out an idea on the bank officers who were the lenders. Would they make loans to publishers who they believed were prudent at an agreed rate if the Ford Foundation would guarantee the loan? Ford thought this was a sensible approach, if they would be allowed to provide supervision. They hoped that after a transition period, the bank and the borrower would be able to develop a normal commercial relationship without a Ford guarantee.

I took this program on the road, returning to each of the publishing groups. After the first two meetings, I was very discouraged. Looking at the audience as I talked, I saw heads bobbing up and down which I believed to be assent. After the meeting, I was barraged by a litany of negative reactions. I discovered that assent was expressed by moving the head from side-to-side the reverse of the Western custom. The publishers were showing me their disapproval. This was an important, if not essential, learning experience in communication. At this point, with a completely negative reaction to what I thought was a good deal, I was ready to go back to the United States.

One of the publishers in Madras invited us to visit holy sites with his family, and as we walked together, he counseled that I was not communicating in a way that was relevant to the Indian culture. I was too American. He gave me an English version of one of the most popular Indian classics to read. The story was told as a fable, but its meaning in real life terms was transparent. I had a "eureka!" moment.

I scheduled a meeting with one of the groups that had been negative and I told this fable:

A farmer who lived in a valley with rich land, below one of the tallest mountains in India, grew fruit and vegetables that were the best in the country. Unfortunately, there were few people in his valley to buy the fruit, but there were many towns with rich people on the other side of the mountain. The farmer had a cart but no mule to pull the cart, so he could not transport his fruit to the markets over the mountain.

A stranger stopped by and sampled his fruit. The stranger enjoyed the fruit, and when he saw much fruit still unpicked, he asked why. The farmer explained that while he had a cart, the village where all the rich people lived was on the other side of the mountain and he had no mule. The stranger said that he would lend the farmer his mule for as many trips as it would take if the farmer would have his brother stay with the stranger as a show of good faith and would promise to buy his own mule with the money he earned and return the stranger's mule. They agreed.

The farmer picked the fruit and vegetables, borrowed the mule, and made the trip over the mountain. He was greeted warmly by the people living on the other side of the mountain. They carried away baskets of food, and he collected many rupees enough to buy his own mule. The farmer returned home, returned the borrowed mule, and, filled with gratitude, continued to grow food and vegetables. The farmer, who rejoined his brother and thanked him for his help, prospered.

While I was telling this fable, I was encouraged as I watched the heads of the people in the audience moving from side to side in assent. They enjoyed the communication in a form that was comfortable for them. I later drew the comparisons between our proposed deal of guaranteeing their loan and the stranger's offer to provide a mule so that the farmer could cross the mountain and earn money to buy his own mule. Word spread of the fable. Indian publishers who became proponents of the plan I had proposed began to tell other publishers the fable, with their own embellishments. This financial model enabled the Southern Language Book Trust to meet its goals. Today, Indian publishing is a thriving and sophisticated domestic and international business. I treasure this experience because it taught me about the importance of communication in a medium and style that is suited to the listener.

With all candor, much more than this fable accounted for the ultimate success of the Southern Language Book Trust. The fable was a pebble thrown into a very large lake, and it caused ripples. What the Southern Language Book Trust did was to bring attention to the value of publishing books. Few of us would have dreamed then that the Indian book industry would flourish as it has. The current Indian book market is estimated in the billions, and there are now about sixteen thousand publishers. India is the third-largest producer of English-language books, superceded only by the United States and the United Kingdom. The literacy rate in India is 61 percent overall (73 percent male). The Indian population is 1.4 billion and growing by an annual rate of 1.4 percent. Indians own more mobile phones (two hundred sixty-nine million) than any other country except China. India has eighty million Internet users, exceeded only by China, the United States, and Japan.

Of course, fables have been used as a means of effective communication for centuries. They have also become best-sellers in today's world. Take, for example, Spencer Johnson's, *Who Moved My Cheese?* It is a thin volume (ninety-six pages) and has four characters, two mice, Sniff and Scurry, and two little people who are as small as mice but look and act like normal people. The fable tells the story of how these characters react to change. Over twenty million copies have been sold to devoted readers, demonstrating how a fable can still be a life-changing experience.

Dog Talk

I do not think Angel would be impressed by the magic of fables. Since we knew very little about what Angel understands before we adopted her, our communication language was created by trial and error and reinforced with treats. Here are the words that move Angel to action or inaction, and I must confide that it is truly a delight to have so few words to communicate so much. Since Angel is fourteen years old, we suspect that her hearing is impaired. It takes her a long time to respond. (On more than one occasion, I have wondered whether her hearing may not be as impaired as we suspect, and that her having us repeat the commands has become a way of her getting more attention and more, bigger, and better treats when she complies.)

GOLDEN WORD/PHRASE	THE MESSAGE
Yes!	Instant affirmation sends a clear signal.
Let's go	Time for resting is over; time to get moving.
Jump	This is the only way you will ever get yourself on the backseat, so leap. Trust me.
Sit	Time to rest now, to restore energy.

Down	Cool it. We will be here for a while until we figure this out
Treat	You did a great job. Here is a bonus for good performance.
Good Dog	Praise, accompanied by a little petting; touching is good.
Bad Dog	Reprimand: This is wrong, but I still love you.
Cross	The road is clear; now move.
No!	Instant reprimand.
That's all	This is all the food I am going to give you from my plate.

Body Language

As with humans, Angel makes use of body language to supplement her understanding. When I say "cross," I point in the direction I wish her to go. When I am petting her ears, I say, "Good dog." She knows the key word, but the synchronization of my movements is also important. When she sees me put on my jacket and hold the leash, she knows it is time to walk; when she sees me get into my pajamas, she knows it is time to go to bed. By looking into her big brown eyes, I can tell if she is well, sad, or in need of affection. And when her tail wags, I know she is happy.

Angel regards barking as an impolite form of communication. However, if she feels that I am threatened, she will bark. It is a formidable baritone bark. And it gets attention. If there is a stranger approaching my house, she will bark to alert me. She knows my regular visitors and appears quietly at the front door, tail wagging to greet them. Paula has two smaller dogs, and, when Angel visits them on the weekend, if they bark, she will join in with a gentle bark, just to be sociable. There are times when Angel appears as though she wishes she could talk. She has a soft, beguiling whimper to let me know that she is in the room and needs attention, not a treat, but a comforting rub behind her ear and under her chin.

Body language is as expressive as words and in some cases reveals emotions that may at times be contrary to the words. Facing danger, a person crying out "I am not afraid' may reveal her true feelings if her body is shaking as she speaks. The conventional concept that a firm handshake shows confidence may be overridden by a facial expression that shows wincing from the pressure exerted.

This is certainly not a new discovery. The use of the body as an expressive tool, *pantomime,* can be traced to ancient Greece and continues to the present. Mime developed early in nineteenth-century Paris through the work of Jean-Gaspard Deburau, who appeared as a silent man in white-face. Mime also played an important part in early motion pictures featuring Charles Chaplin, Harold Lloyd, and Buster Keaton. Charles Chaplin may be the best-documented mime in history.

Experts on body language have identified a wide variety of body parts the face, arms, fingers, torso, legs and feet that carry messages supplementing or modifying spoken language. Professional poker players have identified what they call the "tell." It is an involuntary movement or position of the body that telegraphs a message revealing whether an opponent has a strong hand or a weak one. A tell may be excessive blinking, or the positions of the hands or any other part of the body.

Actors and singers use gestures and body movements to augment their vocal performance. When one sees an Elvis Presley performance, there is very little left to the imagination regarding the message being conveyed.

ALL I KNOW ABOUT MANAGEMENT

A smile is a very important tool to have in one's repertoire. It is often contagious and many times it modifies language. Smiling and saying "You are a tricky one" may be acceptable, but when said without a smile, this phrase might start World War III.

Some actions using the body to convey a message are voluntary. Sarah Palin, the former governor of Alaska and the candidate for vice president in 2008, often looked into the television camera and winked (a conventional flirting device), sending a special message, supposedly to nudge undecided voters. One expert, Jo-Ellan Dimitrius, wrote that Palin's handwringing and poor posture during the ABC interview with Charles Gibson indicated insecurity. Later, a picture of Palin with her mouth open, accompanied by a glazed look as she tried to buy time for a response during a disappointing interview with Katie Couric on CBS News, showed she was stumped by the question.

When Sarah Palin resigned as governor of Alaska before completing her term in office and wrote her memoir, she invited intense press scrutiny. The book she wrote, *Going Rogue*, covered Palin's life before politics, her years in government, and her failed campaign. Deliberately or not, it appeared she was using code words to make her appear "just folks." The Associated Press electronically scanned the book. They concluded that her underlying (and sometimes overstated) message conveyed that she was a "plain person just like you." Palin referred to her husband, Todd, more than two hundred times and used words like *kids, mom,* and *dad* about six hundred times. While Palin may be short on qualifications to be president, she must get high marks for trying to use written language to create a persona.

The Power to Motivate

Managers at all levels use language to lead, reason with, rebuke, reassure and inspire those who look to them for leadership. It takes a special talent to use language to reach the hearts and minds of listeners. Those at a management level should seek to develop a style and a level of communication that can convey the message succinctly and in a memorable manner. Three excerpts from speeches demonstrate this point – the first from Franklin D. Roosevelt, the second from Winston Churchill, and the third from Martin Luther King, Jr.. (The full speeches are available on the Internet, recorded as they were made and in text versions.)

On March 4, 1933, Roosevelt when speaking to a tired and despondent nation, in the midst of the Depression, said,

> "This great nation will endure as it has always endured, will revive and will prosper. So, first of all let me assert my firm belief that the only thing we have to fear is fear itself..."

The words "the only thing we have to fear is fear itself" became a source of inspiration to a nation and have become a part of our culture.

On March 1, 1955, Winston Churchill, preparing to leave the government after a brilliant leadership term, said,

> "The day may dawn when fair play, love for one's fellow-men, respect for justice and freedom, will enable torment-ed generations to march forth serene and triumphant from the hideous epoch in which we have to dwell. Meanwhile, never flinch, never weary, never despair."

The words "never flinch, never weary, never despair" lifted up a nation after a long and painful decade.

On August 28, 1963, Martin Luther King, Jr., standing facing the Washington Monument, with crowds stretching as far as the eye could see, said,

> "Let us not wallow in the valley of despair, I say to you today, my friends, and so even though we face the dif-ficulties of today and tomorrow, I still have a dream. It is a dream deeply rooted in the American dream......I have a dream, today."

King repeated the phrase "I have a dream" eight times in different contexts as he completed his speech. This speech helped keep the dream alive in the struggle for racial equality.

The Internet

In 2009, the Internet celebrated its fortieth birthday. This technology has revolutionized communication. In reality, the tipping point of this new technology was reached in the 1990s when e-mail and sophisticated search engines became generally available. The creation of My Space, Facebook, and Twitter followed and resulted in the creation of social networks, facilitating communication even more.

These phenomena have been augmented by the growth and affordability of the cell phone. It was once said that you could tell who the manager was by finding the person with the BlackBerry or iPhone. This is, of course, no longer true, because these two brands are available to most people. In fact, a market survey by Portio Research reports that half of the world's population are using a cell phone. It was estimated that cell usage in the United States would grow by 66 million phones each year until the end of 2011. The next phase of telephone sophistication is upon us, with smart phones that can store books to read, have a built-in GPS, and are loaded with innovative applications, including live television.

While the formalities of communication will, to a large extent, be conducted via technology-based devices, the most effective communication tool in management is still the face-to-face meeting not by video hookup but in person. E-mail is fast and convenient, but a smile and a handshake (or a hug) get better results. Management is still rooted in the in-person interface of those who have a common interest in seeing the enterprise grow and their fortunes rise with it. As Al Casey demonstrated, you've got to be there.

Coda

THE MOST SPECIAL GIFT HUMANS POSSESS IS, OF COURSE, language. In our best moments, we have used this gift wisely to enrich our culture and refresh our souls. The journey continues as we find new and exciting ways to communicate.

RULE 3

Problem Solving & Decision Making

After more than half a century, the words and thoughts of the leading practitioner of management practices, Peter F. Drucker, remain the wisest and clearest of all evaluations of the relative importance of problem solving and strategic decisions.

In this landmark book, *The Practice of Management,* published in 1954, after intensive study of many major corporations, Drucker wrote: "Whatever a manager does he does through making a decision. The only kind of decision that centers on problem solving is the unimportant, the routine, the tactical. But the important decisions are strategic."

Angel can solve problems and often takes the same steps an individual does - up to a point. Her brain is not robust enough to make generalizations. The human brain is structured to make generalization and associations that enable it to solve problems. Consider Angel. She has been given a place on the floor in our kitchen for her bones. (There is a recessed kick slot between the kitchen cabinet and floor so that it is possible to sweep under the cabinets.) She smells the bone and loves it. She starts to eat it and finds it is slippery. She puts a paw on the bone to stabilize it. She starts eating, and it slips across the floor and into the kick slot. She attempts to use her paws to pry it free. This fails. She growls at the bone - still no movement. She lies down and contemplates. She looks around for help and sees me, her master and friend. She runs back and forth to attract my attention to her dilemma. I retrieve the bone and place it on a rug in a nearby room, where it will be accessible and will not slide. She holds it with her paw and devours the bone.

HERE ARE CLASSIC STEPS IN PROBLEM SOLVING FOR ANGEL:

1. Define the problem: Bone is stuck and I cannot get to it.

2. Look at potential causes (not able to do this; she does not have the ability to generalize).

3. Identify alternatives: Growling did not move the bone; try master.

4. Action plan: Run up and down to get attention and help. Master moves bone to the rug.

5. Monitor implementation of the plan: Keep the bone on the rug.

6. Postmortem: Take bone to the rug next time. (She remembers; she can do this because she is such a smart dog.)

In short, the skillful manager in Angel's world will remember that there will be a problem when trying to eat a bone on a slippery floor, because it probably will get stuck in the kick - plate area and she will not be able to reach it. Next time when she is given a bone, she must carry the bone off the slippery floor and take it to the rug immediately.

Beyond Angel, in the humans' world, because of its importance, there have been a countless number of books and articles on decision making in management.

When reviewed, a consensus of a workable definition for making a successful decision would involve the following process: When faced with a problem that impedes the attainment of a desired goal, (1) ask the right questions to obtain the information needed; (2) identify alternatives; (3) rank the probability of the alternatives in arriving at a successful outcome on a timely basis; (4) make the decision; (5) stay with it through implementation and make modifications when necessary; and (6) do a postmortem to utilize the information gained to aid in making the next decision.

In the end, decision making is like golf; it is a one-person sport. The golfer may seek advice from his caddie, but the golfer is the one who makes the shot and is held accountable on the score card.

Handling Risk

Risk is always present in every decision. In some instances, the fear of the risk immobilizes the decision maker or leads to a postponement of a decision. Don Martin and Renee Martin, friends and clients of many years, have written an important book, *The Risk Takers,* which tells the stories of sixteen entrepreneurs. All of the sixteen entrepreneurs bet their lives and resources that they could make strategic decisions that would lead to success. In most instances, they found a need in the marketplace, had a gut feeling their method would succeed, and proceeded with hard work and perseverance to realize their dreams.

The risk exposure in a corporate environment is less than in a private endeavor; however, it is inherent in every decision, and the manager who is on the spot, admit it or not, is aware of such risk. Management is not for the faint of heart. With practice, and some success, some managers feel that making decisions is the best part of the job.

Perfection is Not Necessary

BOOK PUBLISHERS MADE 285,000 INDIVIDUAL DECISIONS IN 2009 and are expected to continue making decisions at the this rate well into the future. Every book published requires a separate decision, whether it is a book with an investment of three thousand dollars or three million dollars. Publishers pay small, modest, large, and, sometimes, outrageous amounts of money to authors as advances against royalties, (and some of these authors may never have had a book previously published), and then they spend more money for production and marketing, based primarily on their initial subjective evaluation.

The book-selection process starts (as it did with this book) with a manuscript read by an editor, and probably also by a senior editor if a second opinion is needed. Where the advance payment is significant, the book may be read by others in the firm, and in some unusual circumstances, advice is solicited from a major bookseller, as well. Where there have been books in the same genre, sales figures for these books will be reviewed. There are no focus groups or market testing.

A publishing committee, often composed of a senior executive, a marketing executive, the editor in chief, and a financial officer, meets and makes the decisions, book by book, about whether or not to publish the submitted manuscript and what the basic terms of the contract with the author should be. The manuscript is edited, revised by the author, sometimes reedited, polished again by the author, and then copyedited. Once the manuscript is ready for production, the publisher operates as any "product manufacturer" would. A decision is made on retail price, and the book is manufactured, promoted, shipped, and billed to the retail and wholesale customers (who can return the book for full credit if it is a dud).

What is the success rate in this decision-making environment? It varies, based on the nature of the book. In the fiction category, only about 50 percent of the books will get beyond a first printing. (In other categories, this percentage will be somewhat higher.) The half that survive are reprinted and become the "back list," a continuing asset for the publisher.

The book-publishing industry now has revenues of forty billion dollars. It is a mature industry and one in transition. Twenty publishers account for eighty percent of the revenue and report profits that range from seven percent to fifteen percent of revenue. Eighteen of the twenty are publicly held companies. There is also, of course, a significant number of independent publishers that are smaller in size and make a substantial contribution to the industry.

Many other factors are involved in publishing a book, but my point here is that decisions in the publishing industry rest largely on the ability of talented individuals to make judgment calls based mainly on their intuition and experience. To be sure, there are reference points and best practices, but the product choice is made from the gut in the same manner that all risk takers make choices. Book publishing is not unique in this regard. Many creative industries, notably the fashion industry, are successful due to the taste, fancy, and sensibilities that guide the individuals making the decisions.

Watch Out for the Amygdala

THE GREAT PHILOSOPHERS BUILT THEIR THEORIES ON THE basis that all human beings are rational. We were led to believe that if we ask the right questions and analyze the alternatives, we can reach a decision in a rational manner, being rational human beings. According to the latest studies of the brain, this is not altogether true. Our decision-making process is often affected in part by the *amygdala*, a little almond-shaped structure (*amygdala* is the Greek word for almond), a part of the limbic system that is located deep inside the anterior inferior region of the temporal lobe. This is the center for emotions, such as friendship, love, affection, fear, and anxiety, as well as a wealth of other emotions. The best and most crucial decisions require that we use all of the brain.

THE SIX-MINUTE FLIGHT

It is 3:25 P.M. Flight 1539 takes off from runway four at New York's La Guardia Airport with the first officer at the controls. During the ascent, he notices a formation of birds approaching the aircraft at 3:27 P.M., two minutes after takeoff. The plane reaches 3,200 feet, on the way up to 15,000 feet. The aircraft collides with the birds at 3:27:01. The windshield turns dark brown, and several loud thuds are heard. Both engines ingest birds and immediately lose almost all thrust. The captain takes over the controls, while the first officer starts to go through the three-page emergency procedure checklist in an attempt to restart the engines.

At 3:27:36, using call sign Cactus 1539, the flight radios air-traffic controllers at New York Terminal Radar Approach Control. "Hit birds. We lost thrust in both engines. Returning back toward La Guardia." There are more loud bangs, flaming exhaust, then silence from the engines and the odor of fuel in the cabin. La Guardia Tower radios that southeast runway thirteen is available. The captain replies that he is unable to return and

requests permission to make an emergency landing at
Teterboro Airport, in New Jersey. Permission is granted.
The captain now says he is unable to do this, either. He
responds, "We are going to be in the Hudson River." The
aircraft drops to nine hundred feet and ends its six-
minute flight at 3:31 P.M. with a unpowered landing in
the Hudson River. The aircrew evacuates the one hundred
fifty passengers, who are picked up by a number of boats
that rush to the downed airplane. The pilot is Captain
Sullenberg, and the date is January 15, 2009.

According to Jonah Lehner, who worked with the Nobel
Prize-winning neuroscientist Eric Kandel and is the author of
How We Decide we must be able to think with the whole mind.
The stereotype of the unemotional, "just the facts" manager
is, or should be, disappearing from decision making. Captain
Sullenberg made decisions based on the wealth of judgment
he had built up over time. And in the six minutes available
to him, with one hundred fifty lives at stake, he used his emotions and his instincts to assess his options and weigh them,
thereby making a heroic decision. And, in the process, all
three parts of the human brain came into play.

DECISIONS THAT TRY SOULS

Harry Truman was the thirty-third president of the United States. He succeeded to the presidency upon the death of Franklin D. Roosevelt, April 12, 1945. He had to decide whether or not to drop the atomic bomb. There was a sign on his presidential desk: The Buck Stops Here. It did.

Truman was told of the existence of the atom bomb only when he assumed office. Work had begun on creating the bomb in 1939. The decision to use the bomb was examined and discussed by scientists, the military, the cabinet, the secretary of defense and secretary of state without a leak.

By the summer of 1945, given the allied victory in Europe and the intense bombarding of Japanese strongholds, it was believed that the Japanese were, in fact, already defeated and that it was only a matter of time before they would surrender. At a meeting in Potsdam, Germany, on July 26, 1945, Churchill, Truman, and Chiang Kai-Shek issued a demand that Japan surrender unconditionally. Japan refused. Truman had the option of a land invasion, with estimates of high

United States casualties. Truman told the Japanese and the world that the United States possessed a bomb that would devastate cities and kill hundreds of thousands of people. When Japan refused to surrender, the United States bombed Hiroshima, killing 66,000 people immediately (and an estimated 140,000 more over the next five years) and laying waste to 4.4 miles, over two-thirds of the city. Japan still refused to capitulate.

Truman then ordered the bombing of Nagasaki, in which 39,000 people were killed immediately (and an estimated 60,000 more over the next five years) and half of the city was destroyed. It was only then that the emperor of Japan came forward and, in an historic decision, accepted the terms of surrender. In total, it is estimated that the two atomic bombs eventually led to the deaths of approximately 400,000 people.

In making the decision to bomb Japan, Truman rested heavily on the advice of military experts, who felt that an alternative course-nonatomic bombing, followed by an invasion-would cost anywhere from 250,000 to 3,000,000 American and Japanese lives. The use of the atomic bomb is still a highly debated subject, but in the end Truman made the decision that he was asked to make. After he died, his family found a handwritten note in his desk. Written to himself, it said:

> The world is faced with a situation that means either total destruction or the greatest age in history can be its lot. The decision must be made and it must be made as soon as possible. The great nations and the great peoples of the earth have been through trials and difficulties down through the ages. They have fought each other for sovereignty along with explo-ration of their resources.
> All that has been accomplished is a return to old con-cepts and old ideas.

Truman selected the alternative that would potentially save the most lives, but in this note he revealed his higher moral goal, hoping that the dropping of the atom bomb would lead adversaries to reject "old concepts and ideas" and "create the greatest age in history."

Few in management will have to face a decision as mon-umental as the one Truman faced. However, managers in today's world face difficult choices that affect the lives of tens of thousands of people. The decline of the automotive industry and the closing of automotive plants in Detroit has had a major effect on the lives of its citizens. At the end of 2009, despite an official unemployment rate of 10 percent (17 percent if other considerations, such as the number of people who have stopped looking for work, are factored in), there was a much broader problem. The reality is that as much as 45 percent of the population has been affected.

Along with a loss of income, unemployed workers have lost their medical benefits, and many have had to forgo treatment of their illnesses. The large number of home owners who are unable to meet their mortgage payments has resulted in foreclosure and the loss of their homes. Overhead news photographs of the city of Detroit show closed plants rusting away, abandoned homes, rubble in the streets. This scene has been replicated in cities across the United States as government and industry seek an end to the worst recession since the Great Depression.

Look Ahead

Most managers now accept that strategic planning is an essential part of their business lives. This has not always been true. Planning exercises can provide a projection for one to three years, or more, exercises in which a corporate body is examined and decisions are made regarding how to keep it healthy and vibrant. This is a process that seeks to identify goals, put strategies in place to achieve these goals, assign tasks, create milestones to measure progress, and indicate the resources needed.

An essential part of planning is to look back as well as forward and to revisit plans that have worked as well as those that have failed. When a plan works, it is important to celebrate its success. This reinforces the value of planning and encourages those who have been involved in the planning effort. A plan that did not work should be filed away along with the best guess of why it failed.

Many senior managers in small companies resist strategic planning. They feel that all that is needed is a solid budget for the next year and performance that will result in meeting or exceeding the financial goals. They believe that predicting long-range revenue estimates, up or down, will result in making any plan become one built on sand. They feel that guessing about the future is not a useful exercise.

To convert the reluctant planner it will probably take a major disruption, a bad year, changes in technology, and/or stronger competition in their marketplace. Condé Nast Publications is a worldwide magazine-publishing company. Controlling interest was purchased by S. I. Newhouse, Jr., in 1959. The company was founded by Condé Montrose Nast in 1909, when he took over the flagship magazine, *Vogue*. By 1998, the group included seventeen publications, some of which were the largest in their respective markets. Collectively, these magazines had an average circulation of thirteen million issues a month and an estimated readership five times larger than that.

In August 2007, Condé Nast folded the magazine *Jane* and shut its Web site down. In December 2007, the company ceased publication of one of its oldest titles, with a paid circulation of almost one million. After an extensive review by an outside consulting group, Condé Nast was forced in September 2009 to cut 25 percent of its budget, citing a decrease in advertising sales and the transition to a digital business model. On October 5, 2009, Condé Nast announced the closure of four additional publications, *Cookie* magazine, *Modern Bride*, *Elegant Bride*, and *Gourmet*.

The Condé Nast story has been repeated across the magazine and newspaper industries. Legends such as the *New York Times*, the *Los Angeles Times*, and the *Washington Post* have all had substantial losses in profitability and have made staff and other reductions. Two decades ago, the publishing industry benefited as technological changes made it more efficient and economical to print its products. All these industries were late in recognizing that 50 percent of all adults would go online daily; ninety million people read newspapers on the Internet each week.

In February 2004, a Harvard student, Mark Zuckerberg, founded an exclusive social network for Harvard students. It was a huge hit, and within four months, he had thirty more college networks. By the fall of 2007, over one million new users signed up every week, and there were fifty million users by September 2007. While the number will increase, there are over three hundred fifty million users as of this writing. Microsoft invested $240 million for 1.6 percent of a company, making the valuation at that time $15 billion. The company is, of course, Facebook.

For some reasons that will be clear someday, the magazine, newspaper and books industries missed the opportunities inherent in a technological revolution that is still continuing. Planning today requires a manager to put up a periscope and look at the horizon in every direction. The competitive and technological challenges may be hard to see through the fog, but they are always there on the horizon.

The Largest Asset Not on the Balance Sheet

Angel hates summertime. Our house is located on the water in Rye, New York, a suburb of New York City. It sits on a protected inlet adjacent to Long Island Sound, a body of water that flows into the Atlantic Ocean. In late afternoons during the summer, clouds gather, bringing with them thunderstorms, often without much notice. When these storms hit, Angel flips out. No longer a passive, lovable dog, her body shakes, and she looks for a hiding place, usually in a dark corner under a table. Our strategic plan: to look ahead each morning, by checking the daily newspaper and television to see if an afternoon thundershower is likely.

While Angel is freaked out by thunder storms, fireworks frighten her even more. She has tremors, her jaws open, her marked Chow tongue protrudes, and saliva drips from her mouth. Not a pretty sight. There are many beach clubs and an amusement park in the area in which we live, and most have fireworks almost every weekend. The beach clubs add to this mayhem by having fireworks on holidays. On weekends and holidays, we check out the local newspaper and arrange our social schedule to be on hand to comfort Angel.

ALL I KNOW ABOUT MANAGEMENT

Our look-ahead plan: When we see that there is a likelihood of storms or that fireworks are scheduled, we settle Angel down on her bed, turn on the lights in the room, and adjust the volume on the television so that it is really LOUD. If we time it correctly and set the television volume up sufficiently to drown out the thunder or the firework booms and whistles, she will put her head down, bring her two front paws up close to her head, and go off to sleep until the danger passes. Our plan is not an elegant solution to a world-shaking business problem; it is simply looking ahead on a practical level.

As in all plans, some measures do not work. Recently, Angel woke up during a strong thunderstorm because the television was not sufficiently loud. After our normal caressing failed, Angel freaked out and ran in the direction of the garage, whining to be taken for a car ride, her favorite pastime. I thought a ride would divert her attention and quiet her.

I opened the garage, she jumped into the backseat, and I backed out and started driving through the storm, forgetting that Angel always insists on having the back window open so she can thrust her head out to see what is happening. Angel seemed subdued, but she began to whine to indicate her displeasure at not having her window open. Since the driving seemed to be quieting Angel, I finally opened the window. As the window opened, there was a sudden thunderclap and cloudburst. It dumped rain on Angel, whose head was out the window, and before I could close it, another gust drove water into the front seat, and drenching me. We returned home, both of us soaked by the rain. Angel shook the water off, and since the thunder had still not stopped, her shaking returned. Driving around in a heavy storm has been removed from our pre-planning playbook.

We have tried premedicating Angel with pet tranquilizers, but we know how she can react to medication. In order to move her out of anxiety's way, we have tried a change of location, taking her inland, away from our house. We took her to a movie theater (she is a service dog, after all, so she must be allowed to enter the theater), hoping that a darkened environment and music in the background would divert her attention. On the surface, this appeared to be a great idea, because she would be in a darkened room, with the background music of the film masking the thunder and lightning. But Angel became uncomfortable, and squeezed under our seats, finding the objects on the screen and the background music as threatening as the thunder. She rose and forcefully dragged us to the exit. This plan has also been removed from our playbook.

But in spite of these minor setbacks, Angel was instrumental in making me focus on an essential point in decision making. The most important asset not on the balance sheet is people. She is my service dog, assigned and trained to care of me. One of my top priorities is to take care of her. And so it is in strategic planning. I wish to protect her from freaking out in thunderstorms and from the threatening noises of fireworks. What I have learned not to do is put her in the car during a storm with the back window open or take her to the cinema. I need to keep my concern within rational bounds. Well-selected, well-trained, well-paid, well-motivated, secure employees are essential to the success of any business and the viability of any strategic plan. Along with this, a special provision is needed for management succession, so that there is a cadre of experienced players ready to take over positions that become available.

Job security is a crucial issue. Federal and state governments have developed plans to handle short-term layoffs, and it is likely that such plans will include an expansion of health benefits. Both the government and individual employers have undertaken retraining programs to meet the need for new skills in coping with the new technology. With government support employers have been able to offer profit participation and pension plans. It is fair to ask how employees can be made to feel secure when the nation experiences periods of economic instability, but there is not a good answer to this question yet. Disaster planning is still a personal responsibility.

However, what Paula and I do with Angel - try to work it out - also applies to business enterprises. Paula and I do not have to conduct a survey to see what may be changing in technology or the competitive environment; all we need is a calendar and a weather report. We do not need to write the plan and circulate it for comments before we publish our strategy and then advise our shareholders. Our goal is to keep Angel peaceful until the storm or fireworks are over. Instead of an increasing profit goal, our objective is to be gainfully employed and keep this dog happy and healthy. So it must be, first and foremost, with any organization that is to succeed. To come full circle, we find that we need to do some long-range planning about Angel. The SPCA originally told us that Angel was nine years old. Our vet tells us she was older and now may very likely be pushing fourteen years of age. She is still spry, chasing squirrels and rabbits with vigor. But we are looking around now for another golden retriever, younger, who will be there when Angel is gone. We would like Angel II to capture Angel's substance and sensitivity. That's our long-range plan. While Angel may be a bit insecure when she sees Angel II for the first time, I hope to convince her that succession is important for continuity. She should know we will always love and protect her, and in return she should help us show Angel II all of her tricks, because humans and animals have been around for centuries and we stand on the shoulders (backs) of those who preceded us.

RULE 4

Perseverance & Success

Angel loves food, especially bones with meat clinging to them. This usually is dessert and, as far as Angel is concerned, it is better, much better, than the meal. Angel's approach is to attack the bone systematically, first smelling it to establish that the enterprise on which she is to embark is worth her time. Her next step is to chew off the meat, which comes away easily, rest, and then, with her incisor's, relentlessly strip off the sinew that clings to the bone, level by level. No matter how tough the going, Angel persists until the bone is bare. And even then, she will keep the bone on her rug, and, just to make absolutely certain she has not overlooked anything, she will return to it from time to time for another inspection.

Experts, both within the dog world and outside it, agree that perseverance, the will to keep driving forward to a goal, is an essential ingredient in becoming successful in all endeavors. There is a litany of stories to establish that perseverance appears in a broad spectrum of our society, in men and women who, by their determination to overcome challenges, find success.

To define perseverance consider this:

- There was a man who, from age thirty-one until age sixty, had

- Failed business twice,

- Was defeated in legislative races twice,

- Suffered the death of his Sweetheart,

- Suffered a nervous breakdown,

- Lost two senatorial races,

- Lost one vice presidential race,

- And finally was elected president of the United States at age sixty.

That man was Abraham Lincoln. Most challenges are not as great as those faced by Lincoln. Nevertheless, there are those who feel that once rebuffed, trying again is not an option. To Lincoln, failure was not an option. The nation and its values have survived thanks to his service and perseverance.

How to Stop Teaching

Stephen King, was born in Portland, Maine, in 1947. His parents were separated when he was a toddler, and he and his brother were raised by his mother. After spending some of his childhood in Indiana and Connecticut, King returned to Maine. He graduated from the University of Maine at Orono with a B.A. in English in 1970. He met his future wife, Tabitha, when they both worked at the Folger Library at the University of Maine, and they married in January 1971.

Writing was Stephen King's passion. He made his first sale, a short story, *The Glass Floor* to the magazine *Startling Mystery Stories* in 1967. While he was qualified to teach at the high school level, he was unable to find employment. During this time, he and Tabby lived on his earnings as a laborer at an industrial laundry, their income supplemented by the occasional sale of one of his short stories. After he found a position teaching English in the public high school in Hampden, Maine, King continued to write in the evenings and on weekends.

During this period, King, under the pseudonym of Richard Bachman, wrote a handful of short novels that were rejected. In his book *On Writing*, he recalls a conversation with his wife, Tabitha, when he contemplated taking an after-school job as a soccer coach in order to earn additional money, rather than continuing to use this time to write. With Tabitha's support, he refused the job.

King came into my life in 1973, when Doubleday finally accepted a novel, *Carrie*, and published it in the fall of the year. I was then the president of the Times Mirror Book Group and chairman of New American Library, a publisher of paperback novels. The managing director of our English subsidiary, who was on a trip to buy rights for the UK, visited Doubleday and was given a copy of *Carrie*. He fell in love with the book and bought the UK rights for two thousand pounds. Following his lead, NAL bought the book for publication in the United States for $200,000, a substantial sum, but modest in comparison with the prices being paid for major books. On publication of the U.S. paperback edition, I invited Stephen and Tabitha for a celebratory lunch. I sat next to Tabby and asked her what they would do with the money. Her reply was, "I am now going to make Stephen stop teaching and spend his full time writing."

King did continue to write. Since 1973, his production of novels, short stories, audio books, films, *et cetera*, has been prodigious, comprising more than one hundred fifty written works. At one point, during this period, King had to deal with alcoholism and drug abuse. With the support of his friends, he sought help and quit using drugs and alcohol. He has remained sober and drug-free since late in the 1980s.

On June 19, 1999, King was seriously injured in an automobile accident. After a long and painful recovery, he announced in 2002 that he would stop writing because his injuries hampered him, but finally, and fortunately, he recanted. He continues to write, publishing novels, collaborating on musical works, and working with Marvel Comics on a seven-issue miniseries spin-off of *The Dark Tower* series. His latest novel, *Under the Dome* came out on November 10, 2009.

When one comes from a broken family, endures tough economic times, seeks out a college education, holds a full-time job, raises a family, continues to write, handles the rejection of six novels, finally gets published, succeeds, then plunges into and recovers from alcohol and drug addiction, then is critically injured, works through a physical and emotional recovery, and, finally, rediscovers himself, we are looking at a world-class demonstration of persistence.

The Reluctant Publisher

Katharine had a privileged childhood. Her parents owned several homes across the country and left her in the care of nannies, governesses, and tutors in a veritable castle in Mount Kisco, New York and in a smaller home in New York City. She was educated at Vassar and the University of Chicago. Her father, Eugene Meyer, a financier and later a public official, bought the *Washington Post* at a bankruptcy auction in 1933. In June 1940, she married Philip Graham, a graduate of Harvard Law School and a clerk for Supreme Court Justice Felix Frankfurter.

Philip was employed by the *Washington Post* while Katharine raised a family and edited the "Letters to the Editor" column. Katharine was modest and withdrawn; her husband was a handsome and charismatic man. He was made the publisher of the *Washington Post* in 1946, when his father-in-law left the *Post* to become head of the World Bank. The marriage became troubled when Katharine learned her husband was having an affair, but they stayed together.

Philip Graham, a manic-depressive, was hospitalized in 1963. He was released from the facility after a short time but then returned for additional treatment. While at home for a weekend trial release, he committed suicide. Katharine, shy young woman, suddenly found herself president of the Washington Post Company, which included the newspaper, *Newsweek*, and several television stations. She decided to learn about the business by calling in reporters and listening to their concerns. She flew every Monday and Tuesday to cover *Newsweek's* editorial meeting and story conferences. She wrote a friend, "I am quaking in my boots a little." She faced her problems with calm and courage. She persevered until she was equal to the challenges.

Her largest challenge came when she had to make the decision to defy the government and its action against the *New York Times* and publish the Pentagon Papers, the confidential record of U.S. involvement in Indochina from World War II to 1968. She was under tremendous pressure not to publish these documents. Graham recalled in her memoirs that despite financial and legal vulnerability, she decided to publish them. "Frightened and tense, I took a big gulp and said, 'Go ahead, go ahead, go ahead. Let's go. Let's publish,'" she wrote.

Graham presided over the *Post* at a crucial time in history. The *Post* played an integral role in uncovering the Watergate conspiracy, which ultimately led to the resignation of President Nixon. Graham hired Benjamin Bradlee as editor and cultivated Warren Buffett as a shareholder and financial mentor. From a shy, sheltered girl, she persevered and became a major international figure. After a decade as the president of the Washington Post Company, she became chairman of the board, serving in that capacity from 1973 to 1991. Her crowning glory was receiving the Pulitzer Prize in 1998 for her memoir, *Personal History*.

The Outlier

PERSISTENCE IS A QUALITY THAT REQUIRES TIME AND effort, and there may be many turnings in the road before one reaches the goal. Consider this story:

Growing up, I never wanted to be a writer. And then in my last year of college, I decided I wanted to be in advertising. I applied to eighteen advertising agencies in the city of Toronto and received eighteen rejection letters, which I taped in a row on my wall, (I still have them somewhere).

I thought about graduate school, but my grades weren't quite good enough. I applied for a fellowship to go somewhere exotic for a year and was rejected. Writing was a thing I ended up doing by default, for the simple reason that writing could be a job. Jobs were serious and daunting. Writing was fun.

After college, I worked for six months at a little magazine in Indiana, called "The American Spectator." I moved to Washington, D.C. for a few years and eventually caught on with the "Washington Post" and from there came to the "New Yorker."

ALL I KNOW ABOUT MANAGEMENT

The writer is Malcolm Gladwell. It's hard to believe from his early musings that he has written three best-selling books, *The Tipping Point, Blink,* and *Outliers.* He could have told his story in Outliers, in which he developed his theory of success, but he elected to wait until his latest book, *What the Dog Saw,* to slip it into the introduction of this collection of short pieces that had appeared in *The New Yorker.*

In *Outliers,* Gladwell argues that success lies outside normal experience and defies logic. Among other things, it matters where you are born, how long and how hard you work, with whom you connect, and whether you have expended ten thousand hours to perfect your skills.

He uses the Beatles as an example of his theory. They came to the United States in February 1964, starting the so-called British Invasion of the American music scene. They began playing together in 1957, seven years prior to their coming to the United States. Ten years elapsed between the group's founding and its major hit songs.

They entertained in the strip clubs of Hamburg's red-light district, performing long hours (on one trip, they played, five hours or more a night for 106 nights). In total, during their three trips to Hamburg in a year and a half, they performed live twelve hundred times. Gladwell notes that most bands do not perform twelve hundred times during an entire career. It takes a long time to learn how to perform, to develop stamina and a unique style.

Nevertheless, it was a stroke of luck that a Hamburg impresario, Bruno Koschmider, visited England to recruit rock bands to play in Hamburg in what could be called "all-night strip joints." He booked the Beatles for the Cavern Club. And it was Brian Epstein's good fortune that he was at the Cavern Club on November 9, 1961, met the Beatles, and was perceptive enough to extract the group from a contract with a German recording studio, sign them up, and develop them as stars. On February 9, 1964, they attracted eighty million viewers on *The Ed Sullivan Show* - to this day, one of the largest television audiences of all time. After long hours of work, connections, and good fortune, the Beatles were finally an overnight success.

Persistence Plus

Don and Renee Martin performed a valuable service by interviewing sixteen entrepreneurial risk takers and reporting about them in their book, *The Risk Takers* (2010). In most cases, the men and women they interviewed persevered and overcame obstacles to achieve their dreams. These are some of the people who appear in their outstanding book:

Linda Alvarado, founder and CEO of Alvarado Construction. In a male-dominated, industry where most Hispanics are viewed only as laborers, Alvarado ignored the naysayers, became a general contractor, and built the largest Hispanic-owned construction company in the United States. She also became the first Hispanic owner of a major league baseball team the Colorado Rockies.

Paul Orfalea, founder and former CEO of Kinko's, the one time retail leader in copying, printing, and binding services. Struggling to get through college because of his undiagnosed attention deficit/hyperactivity disorder (ADHD) and dyslexia, Paul decided he needed to run his own business to ensure his job security. He grew a one-hundred-square-foot copy shop into a $1.5 billion-a-year company, which FedEx eventually bought for $2.4 billion.

David L. Steward, founder and CEO of World Wide Technology, Inc., the nation's largest African-American-owned company. Subjected to prejudice and segregation as a youth, David learned all about maintaining optimism in the face of adversity at an early age a strength that ultimately served him well as an entrepreneur in the information-technology industry. Starting on a shoestring in 1990, he built a privately held billion-dollar company that provides technology solutions to companies in many industries.

John Paul DeJoria, cofounder and chairman of John Paul Mitchell Systems, maker of Paul Mitchell brand hair and beauty products. He went from broke and sleeping in his car to owning several businesses and residences, including a home in Hawaii. The company has annual salon retail sales of over $900 million. John Paul is also the cofounder of the spirit company that produces Patrón tequila.

Mal Mixon, chairman and CEO of Invacare, the world's leading manufacturer and distributor of wheelchairs and home health-care products. He was thirty-nine years old when he decided to quit his secure corporate job and purchase a struggling business in need of an overhaul. Since acquiring Invacare in 1979, he has led the company to grow its annual sales from $19 million to $1.8 billion.

Tova Borgnine, founder of Tova Corporation, a multi-million-dollar direct-marketing beauty products company whose line includes best-selling fragrances and skin-care products. Speaking no English when she and her mother emigrated from Norway to the United States. Tova grew up as a housekeeper's daughter. After working as a makeup artist, she eventually launched her own brand of beauty products, which she personally helped develop.

There is a long and storied history of men and women over-coming the challenges of prejudice, learning disabilities, dead-end jobs and myriad of other roadblocks in order to achieve their goals.

It seems that perseverance is our heritage. We are wired to dream the impossible dream and make it a reality if we can persevere.

A Final Word From Angel

I admit that Angel is my favorite companion when I go shopping. After testing the circular route, she will, on command, now jump in the backseat and land softly relatively speaking. Once we get going, Angel pokes her head out "her" window, on the right-hand side, and observes passersby. She never barks at dogs that we pass, because she is saying to herself, Why bother when you are walking and here I am riding in a car? When I leave her in the car, I leave her window open, pat her head, stroke her ears, and say, "I'll be back." She stays at the window for a moment and then stretches out on the seat. When I return, she is sound asleep.

ALL I KNOW ABOUT MANAGEMENT

When she hears the door swing open, she gets up, shakes her head, so that the tags on her neck ring, and is ready to go refreshed for the return trip home. These naps do not interfere with Angel's unvarying schedule of finishing dinner, licking her chops, drinking water to wash the food down, and making it to bed by 7:00 P.M. for her obligatory twelve hours of rest (excluding the various daytime naps).

For humans, there are many more issues than sleep and a protective environment. Staying young has long been the subject of philosophers and writers, from Aristotle to the present, and this is not an exaggeration. In the complex management environment, staying young is essential, and there are a number issues involved in remaining so.

Some advise us to disregard nonessential numbers such as age, weight, and height. Song writers advise us to collect friends and put on a happy smile. I, for one, weigh in on the side of those who urge us to keep learning. Going to law school, my childhood dream, which I realized at the age of sixty-one and my subsequent career have, I strongly believe now at the age of ninety-one, kept me feeling young and useful. Norman Cousins, the famous publisher, when incorrectly diagnosed as having a fatal illness, turned to laughter to pull him through. If you look further, there is more to his story than the simple commandment to stay young. Almost every writer of any stature has weighed in on this subject, but to my mind, one of the most touching examples of the importance of staying young is the documentary film, *Young Heart*, in which a chorus of seniors, who range in age from seventy to eighty, are taught the songs of Jimi Hendrix and others. They enjoy the rigors of performing. The film is a command: No matter what your age, stay young at heart.

I am advised by *Angel* that, as far as she is concerned, I have covered the essential, but she informs me that if I take regular naps and stay young at heart, she expects more from me - there is much more to come. She has referred me to her reading on Heraclitus, the Greek scholar who lived in the period from 535 B.C. to 475 B.C., and who is known for the doctrine of change. He said, Angel tells me, that you cannot step in the same river twice because everything flows, nothing stands still.

Books Worth Reading

I HAVE SELECTED, FROM THE MANY BOOKS THAT I ENJOYED in preparing this little monograph, a short list of books I feel are worth reading. If you are interested in management (or in dogs), you will spend many a happy hour reading, as did I.

ALL ABOUT DOGS

Temple Grandin and Catherine Johnson,
> *Animals in Translation* (New York: Harcourt, Inc.
> 2005).

Steven P Hicks, ed., *What Philosophy Can Tell You*
> *About Your Dog* (New York, Open Court, 2008).

Konrad Lorenz, *Man Meets Dog*
> (New York: Kodansha International, 1994,
> originally published in German in 1953).

Elizabeth Marshall Thomas,
> *The Hidden Life of Dogs*
> (New York: Pocket Books, 1993).

Alexandra Horowitz, *Inside a Dog*
> (New York: Scribner, 2009).

Victoria Schade, *Bonding With Your Dog*
> (New York: Wiley, 2009).

Les Krantz, *Power of the Dog*
> (New York: St. Martin's Press, 2009).

MANAGEMENT OLD AND NEW FRIENDS

Peter F. Drucker, *The Practice of Management* (New York: Harper & Brothers, 1954).

Thomas J. Peters and Robert H. Waterman, Jr., *In Search of Excellence* (New York: HarperCollins, 2004. Originally published in 1982).

William F. Baker and Michael O'Malley, *Leading With Kindness* (New York: AMACON, 2008).

Allan and Barbara Pease, The Definitive Book of Body Language (New York: Bantam, 2006).

Jonah Lehrer, *How We Decide* (New York: Houghton Mifflin Harcourt, 2009).

Ken Auletta, *Googled: The End of the World as We Know It* (New York: Penguin, 2009).

Don and Renee Martin, *The Risk Takers* (New York: Vanguard, 2010).

I LEARNED FROM MY DOG

GREAT TRUE-LIFE DOG STORIES

Ted Kerasote, *Merle's Door* (Orlando, Florida: Harcourt, 2007).

Jon Katz, *Izzy & Leonore* (New York: Villard Books, 2008).

Lt. Col. Jay Kopleman, with Melinda Roth, *From Baghdad with Love* (Guilford, Connecticut: Lyons Press, 2006).

Kathryn Miles, *Adventures with Ari* (New York: Skyhorse Publishing, 2009).

Dick Wolfsie, *Mornings with Barney*, (New York: Skyhorse Publishing, 2009).

Mark R. Levin, *Rescuing Sprite* (New York: Pocket Books, 2007).

ABOUT THE PLAYERS

MARTIN LEVIN began career in book publishing in 1950 at Grosset & Dunlap (now a part of Penguin). Starting as the assistant to the assistant sales manager, he rose through the organization to become the COO and a member of the board of directors. In July 1966, he was recruited by the Times Mirror Company, a Los Angeles company that was the publisher of the *Los Angeles Times*, to be the president of the Book Group and a vice president of the parent company. Times Mirror had acquired New American Library, one of the big three paperback houses in the United States, and wished to increase its publishing portfolio. From 1966 until his retirement in December 1983, Mr. Levin became a formidable presence in trade and professional publishing, so that by 1980 the Times Mirror Book Group was the fifth-largest publishing entity in the United States. He also served a term as the president of the American Association of Publishers and was deeply involved in the both the Moscow and Jerusalem books fairs.

When he was sixty-one, in preparation for his retirement, Mr. Levin enrolled at New York Law School. Keeping his day job, he attended night school, graduating in June 1983 and retiring from Times Mirror in December 1983. Mr. Levin passed the bar exam and was admitted to the practice of law in June 1984. He joined the law firm of Cowan, Liebowitz & Latman, P.C., one of the leading intellectual-property firms in the United States in 1985 and shortly thereafter became the co-director of the Mergers and Acquisition division of Cowan.

During his career, he has been deeply involved in the growth of publishing abroad. In 1956 and 1957, he took a short leave from his job to work on behalf of the Ford Foundation in India. In 1976, he was a part of the first delegation of publishers to the then Soviet Union and represented the American Institute of Physics in translating Russian professional journals into English. Later, he and his partner, Robert Halper, assisted the *Reader's Digest* in creating their highly successful Russian-language edition. Also in 1976, he was a member of the first delegation of U.S. publishers to the People's Republic of China.

He was the chairman of the Association of American Publishers from 1981 to 1982 and received the industry's highest honor, the Curtis Benjamin Award, in 1999.

For the last twenty-four years, he has been involved in the M and A work of the law firm and has participated in closing 105 transactions over a broad spectrum of disciplines. He has taught Publishing Law at New York Law School for the last twenty-four years. For the last thirty years, he has delivered a series of lectures during the month of July at the Stanford Professional Publishing Course in Palo Alto, California. His presentation of "My Ten Greatest Mistakes," a landmark lecture, is drawn from his personal experience and is only a small sample of the many mistakes he has made in his almost sixty years in publishing.

PAULA DROST came to the United States from Portugal in 1981, a sixteen-year-old girl without any knowledge of the English language. Over the years, she married, raised a family, celebrated the birth of her first grandchild, and became the rescuer of those who need someone to fill a void in their lives after the death of a loved one. She was the key caregiver for Martin Levin's wife, Marcia. And when Marcia died, Paula vowed that in addition to taking care of her family in Sarasota, Florida, she would do whatever had to be done to allow a very active and involved person, Martin Levin, to continue on. Her talents are many and varied. There is no project, including this one, that is too difficult for Paula Drost, and among these endeavors is serving as Angel's mother. While she excels in such diverse areas as wound care and financial management, Paula Drost reads almost fifty books a year. She has traveled with the author regularly to book fairs in London, Israel, and the United States, attending, in addition, the Stanford Professional Publishing Course and the Yale Publishing Course.

TIFFANY **S**CHWARZ, whose photographs appear in this book possesses, as you have seen, an extraordinary talent. While she operates at a highly professional level in many fields, her ability to capture the soul of a dog on film is extraordinary. Visit her website for more of her wonderful photos: **tiffanyschwartzphotography.blogspot.com**

ALL I KNOW ABOUT MANAGEMENT

Angel is center stage in this drama. You already know a great deal about her. We adopted her from the SPCA shelter in Briarcliff, New York on May 1, 2007 at what we now know to be the age of eleven years and eleven months. Her real age would not made any difference to me even then because I was a vigorous 87 years old and that time. I fell madly in love with her as she poked her nose through the bars of her cage and looked at me with her big brown eyes that said, "take me home."

Angel now lives an exciting life, wintering with Paula and me in Sarasota, Florida and spending the spring and fall in Rye, New York, a suburb of New York City.

In recent months we have noticed that Angel was slowing down; understandable for a fifteen year old dog. One evening we found her lying down, having slipped on a polished floor, her front legs splayed out. No matter how hard she tried, she could not stand. With help, we lifted her to the back of our car and drove her to our vet who advised that extensive tests were necessary.

The next day we took her to a world class diagnostic and treatment facility, the Animal Specialty Center in Yonkers, New York where she received a complete physical and neurological examination including an MRI. The diagnosis was shattering to us. Angel had growth in her brain and a spot on her liver, and as we knew, arthritis of the spine. They felt that medication was needed and after the medication kicked in, exercise and Angel's determination could help. The prognosis was guarded.

While we were distressed, Angel never gave up. She took her medicine and she regained her ability to walk, not as far as before, but at a good pace, and she often rises to a standing position without help. Most of all, she is still full of a love of life and people. Her big brown eyes are bright. We do not know how long this will last, but every day we have with her is golden. Angel's message to all of us is: no matter what the adversity, fight on persevere.

We are prepared for the end when ever it comes, hopefully some time from now. If you would like to see how Angel is doing, go to her web page at www.goldenrulesformanagement.com. To show our love for her we are using the royalties from this book to establish an "Angel Fund" with contributions to the SPCA facilities and to the Animal Specialty Center. If you find it in your heart, join me by contributing to the local SPCA shelter in your area or even better adopt an older dog...you may find another Angel.

—Martin Levin